I read this book in
content is captiva
book filled in the c

MW01251374

the point quickly, but with descriptive words. It is a very easy read. His story is fascinating, but his conclusions are even better. How do we deal with life when it appears that we started out with a disadvantage? Denis gives wonderful, life-giving solutions.

—Steve Long

Senior Leader, Catch The Fire Church (Toronto),
author of *My Healing Belongs to Me* and *The Faith Zone*

The author's central message in this book is about establishing a connection to what is really important—and it may surprise you. As he honestly recounts the events of his life, reader find themselves on a journey that is both nostalgic and relatable, compelling, and at times intense. However, it is also endearing.

I fully endorse this book. It is a relevant work for these troubled times we all find ourselves in because it is a tale of artistic creativity, spiritual connection, and genuine lessons and strategies that you can easily apply on a daily basis to enhance and support your own life.

Daviau's message is this: get connected—to family, to community, and to God. He writes, "The key in all areas of life is to stay close to God. His anointing and grace enables us to live victorious lives… It is my hope that the course of my life will have brought a change in the course of yours." I heartily encourage you to read it!

—Dr. Kevin J. Arnold, BSc, DC
author and chiropractor to elite athletes

Denis's story, found within the pages of this little book, is one of an overcomer. He has overcome physical disability, childhood neglect and trauma, professional challenges, and more. He has enjoyed a healthy marriage to Janet, the love of his life, fathered two lovely children, and managed a success career. He has even designed and made musical instruments! He credits all of these life successes to his faith in the Lord Jesus and the rich benefits of communities of like-minded believers.

Nuggets of wisdom are simply and straightforwardly expressed in this narrative. If you are looking for an uplifting story of victory over significant odds, then I commend to you Denis's testimony.

—Ramesh Naraine

Senior Leader, Catch The Fire Church (Toronto East)

DISCONNECTED

Fractured Family to Unified Community

DISCONNECTED

Fractured Family to Unified Community

DENIS DAVIAU

All Scripture quotations, unless otherwise indicated, are taken from the Holy Bible, New International Version®, NIV®. Copyright ©1973, 1978, 1984, 2011 by Biblica, Inc.™ Used by permission of Zondervan. All rights reserved worldwide. www.zondervan.com. The "NIV" and "New International Version" are trademarks registered in the United States Patent and Trademark Office by Biblica, Inc.™ • Scripture quotations marked KJV are taken from the Holy Bible, King James Version, which is in the public domain.

The content of this publication is based on actual events. Names may have been changed to protect individual privacy.

If you wish to contact the author, please email: denis@thepowerofcommunity.ca.

Printed in Canada

ISBN: 978-1-4866-2171-2
eBook ISBN: 978-1-4866-2172-9

Word Alive Press
119 De Baets Street Winnipeg, MB R2J 3R9
www.wordalivepress.ca

Cataloguing in Publication information can be obtained from Library and Archives Canada.

ACKNOWLEDGEMENTS

THROUGHOUT THE PROCESS OF WRITING, MY WIFE JANET HAS BEEN A constant source of strength and encouragement. I want to thank her for that. Her input has been constant, and she made sure I got my facts straight. She also helped a great deal with the editing process, sitting with me and ensuring I didn't miss anything. I also want to thank my friend, Tiffany Smith, for her help in the editing process. She helped make my language more concise and relevant. I also want to extend a special thanks to Cori Mordaunt, who helped me greatly by asking all the right questions so that I could compile my story accurately.

CONTENTS

INTRODUCTION

HAVE YOU EVER BEEN IN THE MIDDLE OF A TELEPHONE CONVERSATION, pouring out your heart over some issue, only to find out that the person you were talking to is no longer there? Disconnected. Even with our modern mobile phones, this still happens. What is even worse is when you are talking to someone in the same room only to find out that they have completely tuned out. This kind of disconnect is very common. If you have ever parented a teenager, you will know exactly what I mean.

In my line of work, I depend heavily on the Internet. I use it to find out the proper way of doing things. I know several computer languages well enough to use them, but not well enough to know all the precise details. So when the Internet is disconnected, I am lost. In the early days, I had books that explained everything. It took a while to find what I was looking for, but these books got the job done. Now Google can tell me how to do just about anything.

What happens when people disconnect? Close friends are rare. Even less common are those who remain close for thirty or forty years. I have a couple of long-term friends, other than my wife. I don't see them often, but we keep in touch. People will drift away, and occasionally you may have an unresolved conflict that breaks a friendship apart. This can cause great emotional pain. In today's society, unresolved conflict in marriage is common and hurts everyone involved, particularly the children.

What happens when a child is removed from a family? The emotional disconnect produces drastic psychological trauma that affects every aspect of their life. I know this, because I am one. As a child, I was oblivious to all of the trauma. Even in my adult life, I did not realize the effect it had on me.

Then it happened—I witnessed the intimacy between a mother and her five-year-old son. That is when I realized that my bond with my parents had been severed long ago, and I had been stunted emotionally.

Buried in the events of my life is a record of redemption. The process of finding my true identity has taken me a lifetime. My heart is to offer you a message of hope, to help you to look at the broken pieces of your life and give yourself permission to dream of a bright tomorrow.

ONE
The Early Days

I WOULD LIKE TO START OFF WITH A BIT OF CULTURAL BACKGROUND. Both of my parents' families were French-Canadian from northern Ontario. They grew up on a farm and were teenagers during the Great Depression. A lot of people, particularly in cities, were unemployed and there was no government help like we have today.

However, they never lacked anything because they lived off the land. In spite of that, their attitude was filled with a sense of poverty. This affected who they were and how they brought us up. For example, food was never wasted and it was normal to work hard for what you wanted. They also had strong religious ties because of their cultural heritage.

I am the middle of three boys, and the three of us are very different from each other. My older brother is very intelligent and resourceful. I, on the other hand, have a much more creative mind. My younger brother is an independent soul, very gifted but never finding his sweet spot.

Life for me did not start well. Because my mother had polio as a child, my birth was traumatic. To make matters worse, no doctor was present. The nurses did the best they could, but I was left with a damaged hip. Also, because they used the wrong drops in my eyes, I was left legally blind. The good news is that I survived. I was able to learn to walk and I have some useful eyesight.

I don't remember a whole lot from my early years. What I do recall are ordinary things. We lived in an apartment on the second floor of a small building. My older brother and I shared a room. Dad worked in the mine at the time; I am not sure which one, since there are two in the Timmins area where we lived.

He used the radio to wake himself up. The station would start broadcasting at 6:00 a.m., and we'd all wake up to the melody and lyrics of "Oh Canada." I remember going blueberry-picking and eating more than I put in the basket. The family always kept mine separate because I managed to pick as many leaves as berries.

There were days so cold that the car wouldn't start. I am not sure Dad ever missed a shift because of the cold, but I do remember having to walk to church on one of those very cold days.

I recall waking up at 6:00 a.m. one Christmas morning, excited to see my new toys. Mom and Dad always seemed to get the right ones for me. I remember getting our first TV set, which sat in the living room for a month before the station started broadcasting. In Timmins, we had two television stations, one in English and one in French. This was in 1956, so I would have been four years old.

As a young child, I used to stare at the light attached to the ceiling of the kitchen. I would stand in the middle of the floor, looking up and twirling around, my eyes on that glowing fixture. I was told countless times to stop staring at the light.

Still, this theme of staring at light stayed with me. I have a vivid memory of being eight or nine and cupping my hands around a Christmas light, hoping to capture a little of it. I never caught any, but I still love staring at the lights at Christmas time. While ordinary for most people, this was magical for a child with vision problems!

We often travelled to visit relatives in various towns around Timmins. Inevitably, we would come home late, so I would fall asleep in the rumble seat of our Volkswagen Beetle. The sound of the engine lulled me to sleep.

I had a very good singing voice as a child, but I was extremely shy… so much so that one time, when asked to sing for relatives, I did it while hiding behind a door the entire time. I also vaguely recall attending a Christmas party put on by the Canadian National Institute for the Blind (CNIB). Henry Kelneck came with his band, and somehow they got me to sing "Rudolf the Red-Nosed Reindeer" into the microphone.

When I turned five, everything changed. In the 1950s, there was a real stigma about being visually impaired. The school systems didn't know how to handle blind students, so attending a local school wasn't a good option. As a result, my parents decided to enroll me in the Ontario School for the Blind in Brantford, eight hundred kilometres from home. I attended there for the next three years. It was an English school, and until then I'd only spoken French, but I did manage to learn enough English while attending the school to get by.

The first time I went, my mother took me there by train. I had no clue what was happening and the first months were difficult. I was a very angry boy and wasn't even sure why. Yes, I had friends—all with various levels of disability—and amazing caregivers, but they weren't family.

A funny thing I remember is that I thought it was strange for a woman to walk without a limp, because my mother had a very noticeable limp from having had polio as a child. To me, Mom was normal and the rest were not.

I only saw my family for two months in the summer and two weeks at Christmas. I don't remember a lot about that time except for ordinary things like learning the multiplication table and the strange food I had to eat. I was taught braille like the rest of the students; however, I could see well enough to look at the page and read instead of feeling the dots.

The school was well regimented. Everyone got up at the same time, ate meals together, and went to bed at the same time, all under the care of the staff. We were taken to Mass every Sunday, no matter what the weather was like. We walked in lines, two by two. One time, one of my mittens got caught in a fence; the line wouldn't stop, so I lost the mitten. For a young child, this was traumatic.

I don't specifically remember the train trips, four per year, but I do vaguely recall one year when it was very cold at Christmas. The train was significantly delayed and we were freezing. Somehow, I still love travelling on the train, and I even stop to watch the public transit trains when they pass.

I went to the school in Brantford for three years. After completing Kindergarten, Grade One, and Grade Two, the authorities decided I was not suited to that type of school because they thought I could see well enough to attend a regular school.

That summer, we moved from our apartment to a house on Carling Avenue. I don't remember moving day. Mom had won an electric dryer at a bingo game, and until we moved it sat in the apartment's kitchen, holding our canned goods because there was no way to hook it up.

In the summer of 1961, my little brother was born. That September, the local creek overflowed and flooded our basement. The damage was extensive. Anything electrical in the basement had to be repaired or replaced, including the new dryer that had just been installed. What a summer that was for Mom and Dad between moving, having a new baby, and enduring the flood.

The transition to public school was difficult. Not only did I have to make new friends in the midst of being so different from everyone else, but I also had to switch from English to French. I had a lot of trouble with blackboards and reading and needed to sit up front, really close to the teacher.

Up until Grade Seven, I did well and could keep up with the work. I even skipped Grade Six because there were too many of us, and the top students were put into a combined class for sixth and seventh graders. Mademoiselle Botchere was an amazing teacher. She was kind and compassionate and knew how to bring out the best in her students.

During those days I was taught Catholic dogma, and we had to learn the catechism. What impacted me from this was all the rules. I seem to remember that there were around seven hundred dos and don'ts. I was conscious of the meaning of sin and hell. I wasn't taught about a relationship with God, only what I had to do to stay in His good books.

First communion was a significant occasion. I think I was nine years old. I wore a suit, probably for the first time in my life, and my parents took pictures. I also remember going to Mass every day during Lent. I had it memorized, word for Latin word, not really understanding any of it. It was during that time—around 1965—that they switched the liturgy from Latin to French.

I loved to participate in sports activities of all kinds. I was terrible because of my poor eyesight, but I still loved it. I was always the last one picked when teams were chosen. I don't think that bothered me, as long as I could participate.

I loved playing baseball. I struck out a lot, but the ball went far when I managed to connect. I remember getting a hit one day that went all the way to the fence. A sure double, but I could not find second base and was tagged out. It sounds funny now, but I was exasperated.

I remember playing baseball with my brother in the backyard until Dad built the garage back there. We made up our own rules so the two of us could have a fun game, but hitting the ball into the neighbour's yard was a problem because of the big dog who lived there.

We also played a lot of pick-up hockey in the wintertime, either at the school rink or on the road. I was on a team and played defence since I could hardly skate. I adopted what I thought was a defensive position. As little kids, hockey was a pack sport. There was always a pack of players moving around the ice with the puck in the middle. I thought it was okay to stay out of the pack and wait for the puck to come my way, but the referee would ask me what I was doing.

"I am playing defence," I would reply.

He would tell me to get in there with the rest of them.

We didn't wear helmets. In fact, except for skates and sticks, we had no equipment at all. Even the goalie had no significant protection. One day, one of the guys was in the net when the puck came flying at his head. He ducked out of the way, allowing a goal. I don't remember anyone getting seriously hurt.

The rinks had to be shovelled by hand. We had no snowblower or Zamboni. If you wanted to use the rink, you had to shovel, period, although each outdoor rink was equipped with a warming hut complete with a wood stove. I assume some adult kept the fire going on those cold days.

Somewhere around the age of eight, I was introduced to Meccano. Meccano consists of a variety of metal pieces, wheels, nuts, bolts, and washers, and one of my cousins had a whole box of it. Mom and Dad bought me a couple of sets, and we ended up getting my cousin's collection as well. I would create my own toys with it—cars, airplanes, whatever. I lived in an imaginary world, playing mostly by myself at home. I was constantly losing some of the tiny parts, so my Mom had the challenge of buying more.

Over time, I also became interested in electronics and radio. This interest started when my parents bought me a crystal set for Christmas. With this, I could listen to the local stations. Being a curious type, wanting to understand how it worked, I learned from library books and magazines that I bought at Radio Shack. I even built a primitive radio with a coil of wire, a razor blade, and a piece of lead from a pencil. I probably found out about that from a magazine.

This love of electronics and radio grew into a passion, and it eventually led to college and a career.

Having a vivid imagination has served me well over the years. It started as play in the early days and developed into an important component of who I am. The ability to see beyond the natural is truly a gift from God.

TWO
Years of Illness

I WAS TEASED AND BULLIED MERCILESSLY AT SCHOOL FOR EIGHT YEARS. During this period, I learned that I could punch my way out of difficult situations because I was a little bigger than others.

One day, the tough guy of the school came after me for one reason or another. At one point he tried to kick me, and I grabbed his leg and flipped him over. He instantly changed his mind about whatever was bothering him and we became friends.

This peace didn't last too long. By the time I hit high school, I had no friends and continued to be tormented by bullies. This made me very reclusive and I wanted to give up.

In eighth grade, when I was twelve or thirteen, I developed a condition that caused bleeding in my bowels. Doctors didn't have a clue what caused it, so my parents drove me to the Hospital for Sick Kids in Toronto and left me there.

Once again, I found myself in a strange and lonely place. On my first visit, it seemed as though I was there for a month. The condition settled, and after a gazillion tests they sent me home. I missed a month of school.

But after experiencing the same symptoms, I eventually returned to Toronto for a second visit. The condition settled again and they sent me home, but I had missed another month of school.

I was okay with being in the hospital. There weren't any bullies, just a lot of really sick children. One boy, also from Timmins, had leukaemia and had been in the hospital for a long time. When his mother came to pick him up, he was overwhelmed with emotion. I later learned that he did not survive.

It was in the hospital that I first began to enjoy listening to music. There was a room on the top floor where the older children would gather in the afternoon during nap time and in the evening. They had this cool stereo with a big wooden cabinet, and I thought the sound was amazing. I loved the big-band music.

The third time I had symptoms, the doctors decided to keep me in the hospital in Timmins. This time, they took a more direct approach and opened me up to see what was happening. They found the issue and fixed it, but I was incoherent for four days after the operation.

Through it all, Dad came to visit me every day. We would play cards and chat. Unfortunately, I missed about six weeks of school, but I got better.

Needless to say, my grades took a beating. I continued to have a lot of trouble in school with blackboards and reading. I was really hopeless in shop class, but I loved science and geography.

Deeply discouraged, and broken from the years of bullying, I needed a change. After completing tenth grade, I asked to be sent back to the School for the Blind.

THREE
Back to Normal

I DON'T KNOW WHAT PROCESS MY PARENTS HAD TO GO THROUGH TO enroll me, but thankfully they got me in. I remember the train ride to take me back to Brantford. It was September 1969 and I was sixteen. All the students going to the school travelled on the same day.

As the train continued south, more kids boarded and I distinctly remember the Bellemer brothers from Val Gagne. There were four of them, all visually impaired. We chatted and hung out together all the way during the overnight trip. I remember expressing a desire to learn to play the saxophone.

The new environment was good for me in many ways. First of all, the bullying stopped because the institution did not tolerate that kind of behaviour. I was far better off than most of the others, being just partially impaired by comparison, and for some reason I didn't miss my family. Maybe the early years of being away from them had disconnected me, and I never really reconnected.

I met a lot of people who deeply impacted my life during those two years. The staff was excellent and the teachers were extremely dedicated to our well-being.

For the most part, I enjoyed the classes, except for history, which I had no interest in whatsoever. I still don't care much for the past. During those days, I was allergic to ragweed, which became a problem in the fall, and had to take antihistamines. Back then, there was only one kind of medicine, the kind that made you sleepy, so I'd usually fall asleep in history class. I eventually dropped the subject entirely, as it was optional.

We had lots of free time and plenty of things to keep us busy. The routine was the same every day. The staff would wake us up by banging on the doors, after which the bathroom quickly became crowded. At first I found it strange that there were no doors on the stalls, and the shower was just one big open area without any privacy. Of course, most of the students couldn't see anything, so it didn't matter. That took me a while to get used to.

All the meals were served in the dining hall, with everyone eating at the same time. The food was okay for mass-prepared bulk food. We had designated seating and the staff served us. If we wanted something, we simply raised a hand.

The campus sat on a large property with lots of open spaces and walking paths. The boys' dormitory was on one side, the school buildings in the middle, and the girl's dormitory on the opposite side. Everything was conveniently within a ten-minute walk.

Music lessons started right away. Although I would have preferred to learn the saxophone, I was assigned to the clarinet. An entire section of the school was devoted to music. They even had soundproof practice rooms where we could make as much noise as we wanted to. Each room had a piano, as many students played that instrument—and some were quite talented. These rooms also accommodated students who were learning piano tuning. The school had both an orchestra and a choir. While the orchestra was challenging to listen to, but the choir was amazing, winning competitions every year.

During our free time, we had plenty of opportunities to get to know each other with frequent conversations. Ken, an older student, had lost his sight as a teenager and hadn't completed high school. He had the most amazing baritone voice—boy, could he sing. We became close friends almost right away and he became a great encouragement. He had a depth of faith and conviction I'd never seen before. I knew there was something different about him, but initially I didn't know what it was that made me hunger for what he had.

In October, Ken introduced me to faith in Jesus. I'd never heard that I could have a personal relationship with Him. Ken explained to me that a relationship with God was not based on what I did, but only on what Jesus did. I was keenly aware of my many inadequacies, and I was ready for the message of salvation by grace, which I accepted immediately. It took several years for me to fully understand what it meant to have a relationship with Jesus. Freedom from the guilt of sin is one thing, but true freedom only comes from a living relationship with God.

In Grade Twelve, we had a new music appreciation teacher when Mr. Smail retired after many years of teaching. He had been a favourite of many of the students. The new teacher was also good, but not the same. One day, he asked the question, "Why does so-and-so use loud chords at the end of his symphonies?" My quick retort was, "To wake up the people so they could go home."

Needless to say, I was not his favourite student. On more than one occasion, my inappropriate and untimely comments landed me into trouble.

One of the funniest things I remember was seeing blind kids play hockey. Seriously! We didn't use a puck back then, but rather a tin can. Everyone had protective gear, and those who could see a little had a definite advantage. These games followed the same pattern as the other games of my youth—a pack of kids skating around with a can in the middle, trying to score in a small net, guarded by a boy who could not see.

One thing I learned from these guys was to never stop trying, regardless of circumstances.

Another example of this never-give-up attitude was the wrestling team. This was not the stuff you see on TV but rather Olympic-style Greco-Roman wrestling. We had an excellent coach who instilled confidence in us. Where this winning attitude really came out was during the citywide tournament. We participated alongside the regular schools of the area. There was never any sense of our team being "disabled." Our boys won their weight classes because they were good.

After high school, I decided to go to college because I thought university would be impossible for me due to the amount of reading required. To earn credits I needed in physics and chemistry to get into the college program I wanted, I had to do another year of high school. I enrolled in the English Catholic school, which was only four blocks from my home in Timmins. In this environment, there seemed to be a much more respectful attitude. I did not experience any bullying that year. Getting those two credits was a breeze because I loved both subjects. I also found that the teachers were very approachable and easy to relate to.

My faith did not grow much that year. I was still very intimidated by my parents and their strict dogma. One thing I did do during that time was read the Bible. I continued to go to Mass with my family. The content of the liturgy was good, but because it was always the same it didn't mean anything to anyone. I remember being reprimanded by my dad one Sunday for tapping my foot during one of the songs. Deep inside, I had a joy that I could not escape or explain.

FOUR

College, the Great Awakening

I SPENT THREE YEARS IN KIRKLAND LAKE GETTING A DIPLOMA IN Electronic Technology. Yes, I did it. I graduated with honours. Those were three wonderful years. The events of those years changed me in many ways, mostly because of the people I hung around with, not only the students. I associated with a wide variety of locals, a community of believers from many different congregations, each contributing and giving to each other.

My first semester in college was shaky financially. I managed to pay for my books and tuition from what little savings I had. My monthly income was only ninety dollars a month, fifty of which went to pay the rent for a small, one-room apartment. The remaining forty was the amount I had to live on, so my diet was not very good—Kraft Dinner, wieners, and beans were my staples. I didn't even have a TV, which I really missed, and I listened to the Canada-Russia hockey series in 1972 on a small transistor radio.

One day in early October 1972, everything changed. It had been three years since I first accepted Jesus's salvation message. I hadn't done much with this except read the Bible. Ken had been a great example to me, but for the most part I was still a timid little boy living my way. I hadn't ever publicly displayed my faith in Christ.

What I needed was a church, and I knew it. I found what I thought was the *kind* of church that Ken attended. I remembered that he went to a Baptist church. I did not know that there was more than one denomination that called itself "Baptist," so I found one and went for the first time that day. What a day! I don't remember the music, the sermon, or even the pastor's name. What I do remember is how warmly I was greeted and embraced by strangers. I was welcomed into a family—a loving, living community.

They invited me to attend the community service that evening. In that small town, four or five of the churches had a common service in the evening since none of them had enough attendees for their own services. This allowed me to connect with many believers.

My circumstances changed almost immediately and three very significant things happened within a week or so.

First, I applied for sponsorship at the local Manpower Retraining program and found out that I was accepted. They reimbursed all my tuition fees and book expenses. The sponsorship also meant that I had a much higher living allowance.

The second thing had to do with my accommodations. As a result of my connection with the church, I met Mrs. McDonald. This sweet little old lady offered room and board for students at the college. Since she didn't have a student that year, she offered me a room, so I had a new place, in a house, with her and her disabled daughter.

The third thing that happened was this—I had a strange skin condition on my fingers that caused them to crack and bleed. I never found out what it was, probably because I was too scared to find out. Around this time, that condition disappeared, seemingly overnight. It is amazing what happens when you make room for the Lord in your life.

I continued to live in the McDonalds' home for the three years I was in college. During the four-month summer break, I always had a job. One summer I worked for the regional telephone company and was positioned in North Bay. While there, I learned a lot about how the telephone system worked. The work I did there was for the most part menial but was a good introduction to the state of communications at the time. So much has changed in the technology since then. This turned out to be relevant to my career as I ended up working twenty-five years for different telephone companies.

Pastor David, the pastor of the Baptist church I was attending, was an odd fellow, not at all like the other pastors in Kirkland Lake. Since I needed a father figure in my life, I gravitated towards him. I got to know him and his family quite well. What really impacted me about being in that Christian community, and particularly Pastor David, was that I was accepted and valued as a person.

It was through them that I went to a convention in Hamilton one year. The convention was held at the university, and we were housed in the residence there. I remember two things from that weekend. First, the bathrooms in the residence were shared by both men and women, which I was very uncomfortable with. The other thing I recall, although not in great detail, was a one-hour session called "Life in the Spirit." After that session, I was filled with joy and the power of the Holy Spirit. I was so excited.

After returning home, I played the guitar and sang in the Spirit for the first time. That sense of joy and power stayed with me, particularly when I played and sang. Pastor David also regularly prayed in the Spirit. This had gotten him into hot water several times because the denomination he belonged to didn't believe in this.

Playing the guitar was not new to me, but singing in the Spirit was. This changed the way I worshipped. I began playing in my teens, on my mother's old Harmony archtop guitar. I got a booklet of chords and taught myself to play, and that has stayed with me. I studied classical guitar after I got married, which I'll discuss in further detail in a later chapter.

During those days in Kirkland Lake, I became familiar with the music coming out of the Toronto Catacombs. This was a gathering of young people in the late 60s and early 70s who met in St. Paul's Anglican Church at Bloor Street and Jarvis in Toronto. This gathering was radical for its time and attracted a lot of young people, and they produced songbooks and tapes of their original music. I am not sure how I got the songbooks and tapes. I just remember that they were given to me. These greatly impacted my view of worship music.

Doctor George and his family were also very influential in my life while I lived in Kirkland Lake. He was a professor at the college. He also was a father figure who mentored me in my faith in many ways. He and his wife had home meetings every week. I don't remember any of the content or format, but I do remember the sense of family, with each person bringing their joys and challenges. A genuine care and concern for each other developed as we talked and prayed through each situation.

After I graduated, I had hoped to get a job right away, but that didn't happen. I waited around in Kirkland Lake for the summer, working odd jobs to supplement my meagre income. The Manpower

Retraining sponsorship had ended, so the only income I had was the disability allowance from the government.

By late August, I had to move back to Timmins to live with my parents. I hadn't talked to them about my faith, as I was totally intimidated. It seemed to me that the Catholic way and the Protestant way were incompatible, and switching was not something one did. Is one right and the other wrong? But back then, it was a big deal to me. I wrote them a letter, which was all I could bring myself to do. Their response was quick and clear: "You live the way you want to, and let us live the way we want to." Somehow I had thought things would be different, and they would be open and understanding of the change in my life.

In the summer of 1975, I decided to have an operation in the hope that my sight would improve. I was put on a waiting list for a suitable cornea, and in November I received the call that they had one for me. The operation was done at Toronto General Hospital.

After the operation, I found myself in a room beside Bill, an older gentleman who'd had cataract surgery. Back then, cataract surgery was a big deal and you stayed in the hospital for a while, not like today when you are in and out in a few hours.

While I was in the hospital, I called my friend Ken, who came to visit me, bringing a portion of his braille Bible to read. Ken was completely blind and got around with a white cane. His Bible was a massive collection of thirty volumes of letter-sized sheets of paper. Each volume was two inches thick.

My desire to have the Bible read to me, along with this act of kindness by my friend, left a deep impression on Bill.

Bill was the owner of an engineering firm in Toronto. Knowing that I needed a job after I recovered, Bill offered me a job in his company.

The operation was a success, but my sight didn't improve.

I remember going for an interview at Bill's company and they wanted to make sure I could see well enough to do the job. So in March 1976, I started as a computer operator. I don't think I had much contact with Bill after that.

FIVE

The Stone Jungle

I MOVED TO TORONTO IN MARCH 1976 AND HAVE A CLEAR MEMORY OF standing in the courtyard near city hall, thinking, *This is a jungle, a place that I thought I would never want to be.* Yet here I was. Work had brought me to Toronto, and the city held on to me for a long time.

Eventually, I would venture to the suburbs. Only after my employer permitted me to work at home did I escape this stone jungle.

I had no place to stay, and it took me a couple of weeks to find one. Because I had regular contact with a CNIB case worker, I knew they had a residence on Bayview Avenue where I could stay for a daily fee. They provided breakfast, dinner, and a room. I travelled back and forth to work by TTC. This was free for me because the CNIB provided me with a pass. All blind people registered with the CNIB in Toronto are given this concession.

Work wasn't difficult to adapt to. I don't recall too much about the initial training, but generally the first year was mechanical—loading punched cards, printer paper, and data tapes. I used my spare time to learn how things worked. I quickly figured out how to program in more than one computer language.

I learned so much on my first job. Because of my understanding of electronics, I was able to quickly learn computer programming. This established my carrier path and to this day, I still do a lot of programming.

Beginning the first week in Toronto, I started to attend the Thursday night meeting of the Catacombs. I had friends in Timmins who knew about the meetings and one of them gave me her son's number. Peter, one of the many young people connected with the group, was glad to pick me up and take me there for the first time. I was greeted and welcomed into this amazing family. It was as though I inherited one hundred brothers and sisters all around my age. By then, the church had changed its name to A Christian Church on a Hill and was no longer led by the founders Merv and Merla.

I lived in a basement apartment in the north end of the city. From there, it was a fifteen-minute walk to the bus that took me to work. There were grocery stores and a laundromat close by. The McDonalds at Bathurst and Steeles, a Jewish area complete with bagel shops, was the best in the city. My budget was tight, but the occasional Big Mac wasn't out of the question and life was comfortable enough. I asked Dad to ship my belongings to me—a bicycle, a TV, and a few other things, and I stayed there for a year.

Initially, I attended a denominational church on Sundays and then the Thursday night meeting downtown. I quickly lost interest in the regular church and started attending the Sunday services of A Christian Church on a Hill, led by Pastor Jim. The culture was different from anything I'd experienced before. This community of believers was a family, a true community, the likes of which I haven't seen since.

Sunday was a true family time. We met in the afternoon, and after a time of teaching we'd have a meal together. Everyone would bring something. We were organized in tables, which were each headed up by a church leader. No one was left out. After the meal, we helped with the clean-up and set-up for the evening worship service.

This sense of community extended far beyond Sunday dinner. It was common for families to take singles into their homes or for groups of singles to share an apartment.

Learning to live together brought a new set of challenges. For example, one of the guys I shared an apartment with was not a morning person. Asking him questions in the morning like "How did you sleep?" usually produced a grumpy answer. I was accustomed to doing things on my own. Adapting to living with others was a challenge, like getting groceries and preparing meals. There were also differences in personality and cleanliness standards.

The musical portion of the worship was also very untraditional. In the style of the early Jesus movement, we sang a lot of scriptures. What a great way of memorizing the Word. Thousands of songs were written because there were large numbers of songwriters in the congregation. A lot of us wrote only one or two songs that made it to the stage, but others were prolific writers. New songs were presented to the worship leaders—and if a song was "good," it would be brought to Mae, who chose which songs to use in the services.

The music was more elaborate than anything I'd previously experienced. In addition to songwriters, there were many musicians in our midst. We had guitars—lots of them—and a violin, flute, trombone, piano, and drums. Yes, in the 70s, drums in church. We even had an amazing organ player. Dancers also participated in the worship team. Being multitalented, I had the opportunity to occasionally play recorder and mandolin. I also wrote several songs.

Two things stick out in my mind during that season. First was the outreach at Christmastime. We set up a worship experience in the Royal Bank Plaza and performed a lot of Christmas music, with instruments and dancers. We brought our own sound system and lights, and it was quite a production. It was memorable. Was anyone impacted by that? I don't know, but we were.

The other thing that impacted many of us were the mission trips. Along with twenty-three others, I travelled to China in 1979. China had just opened its borders to western tourists, so it was a great opportunity not only to travel to an amazingly beautiful country but also make an impact on some of its residents. We'd carefully prepared by learning a little Mandarin and Cantonese, memorizing basic phrases to help us get directions and ask for help. We also practiced songs.

Our trip took us first to Hong Kong, where we spent two or three days. Hong Kong was very interesting. The city was all bustle, 24/7. It seemed like there were people and stores everywhere. One very interesting thing we did was go on a bus tour of some of the poor areas of the island. There was a lot of poverty. In places, villages had been built on the side of a mountain. It was also interesting to watch the planes land at the airport, which was literally an airstrip bounded by mountains and ocean.

It was in Hong Kong that we met our Chinese contact, Lisa. She had been a student in Toronto and had attended our fellowship. She would not travel with us because of the threat of persecution from the Chinese authorities.

From there, we travelled by train to Guangzhou. I remember waking up the first morning to the continuous honking of horns, and it sounded like a traffic jam. Looking out the window, I could only spot a few cars and ten billion bicycles. That was how most people got around.

The hotels were primitive compared to North American standards. No luxuries, just plain rooms. I even recall one bathroom where the stalls just had a hole in the floor. But we were not there for comfort; we were there for the people of China.

Everywhere we went, we attracted crowds as we brought out our instruments and started singing "God Loves the People of the World" in their language. In 1979, the Chinese people were not used to seeing North American tourists, let alone those who sang to them in their language. We were very unusual to them, thus the crowds. We also handed out Bibles and other Christian materials.

During our stay in Guaylin, we went on a boat cruise on the Li River. This was a powerful experience as we sang, danced, and worshipped. I'm sure that seeds of revival were planted as we worshipped in the midst of the beauty of this land.

One of the highlights happened near the end of our time there. When we were in Shanghai, we visited the state-run church. They put us in a balcony, off to one side. To our amazement, they started singing, in Mandarin, "I Am So Glad that Jesus Loves Me…" We knew this song, and we sang along with them in their language. It was powerful.

I was deeply impacted by this trip. I'd never travelled outside of Ontario, having lived a pretty sheltered life. Seeing these multitudes and their hunger for something bigger made me appreciate what I had. I was also left with a great love for the Chinese and a longing to see them experience the freedom to worship.

SIX

The Ladies of My Life

IN GRADE TWELVE, I FELL DEEPLY IN LOVE WITH NADIA. SHE WAS A beautiful young woman—also visually impaired—from a well-to-do family in Toronto. We were both serious about a long-term relationship, but it didn't work out. She had planned to tour Europe that summer with her family and asked me to come along. My parents put the brakes on that real fast. I was expected to stay home and look after my little brother.

Who knows where life would have taken me if I had gone away with her that summer?

Before my trip to China, I'd dated several girls, some casually and others a little more seriously. I was still quite timid and always felt uncomfortable around them.

I dated Beth for several months; however, she broke it off because, according to her, something was missing.

After my trip to China, everything changed. For some reason, I was a lot more relaxed with who I was, probably because of the love and acceptance I had been shown during the trip.

Then I began taking an interest in Janet.

I first noticed Janet at a wedding shower where she was helping with the gifts (I even took a candid picture of her). Here was this beautiful young woman whom I found incredibly attractive. I got to know her through casual encounters and found that her tender-heartedness made her even more attractive, although it took a long time for her to take an interest in me. We spent a lot of time talking about life and acceptance.

One day, we met at Shoppers World and talked for hours in the rain.

Another evening, in September 1980, I told her that I loved her. Her reply was, "No, you don't." She wasn't ready to hear that because of past hurts, but I didn't give up—I continued to pursue her. She never pushed me away but seemed to keep her emotional distance from me.

Then it happened. We were planning to see the movie *Song of the South*, a Disney animation. Before the movie, we had dinner in the cafeteria in the Simpsons building at Queen and Yonge. Near the end of our meal, I told her that I really cared about her. Suddenly, her heart ignited, and from that moment on we were inseparable. She went from keeping her distance to being close.

It was a dramatic change. By February 1981, we were engaged. The day I proposed to her, I was nervous and fidgety, and she could tell I had something to say.

"Spit it out," she said. She has always been bold and direct.

So I asked, "Will you marry me?"

"Yes, but when?"

We chose August 15, 1981. The next six months were a blur with all the preparations that needed to be done.

During that time, Janet was living far away, and at the urging of several people she started taking driving lessons. Even with all the engagement activities, she attended Howard's Driving School. Mrs. Howard was a sweet little old lady, full of faith. She, along with our friends Byron and Linda, instilled enough confidence in Janet that she got her driver's licence by May.

We bought our first car, a Toyota Tercel, mostly on credit. The interest rate was nineteen percent for that kind of loan and we quickly realized that it made no sense to pay such a high rate when we had money in our savings account. By November, after the wedding, we'd paid off the loan. We also bought all the furniture we needed and arranged an amazing honeymoon to the Hawaiian island of Maui. We paid for everything, thanks mostly to my wonderful Janet, who was a diligent saver. Imagine, starting off a marriage debt-free!

I would like to publicly thank our best man and maid of honour, Don and Leona, for all the help they provided. They served us in whatever capacity we needed them for, such as picking dresses for the bridesmaids and many such things. They also encouraged and supported us throughout the process.

In 1981, seven couples from our church had weddings, so everyone was busy. Despite this, we quickly found the venues we needed. The reception was at Westbury Hotel in the Bloor and Yonge area, and the wedding took place at a small church at York Mills and Yonge. The ceremony was beautiful. The music was provided by several of the church musicians and singers. In addition, there were several worship dancers in matching dresses. I can still picture Janet in her wedding dress. She was stunning.

Mom, Dad, and my brother Eugène came for the wedding. I remember Dad commenting that they were deeply impacted. They had never seen anything like that before.

The reception was also exceptional. We had seventy-five guests—some family, and a lot of friends from the church. The meal, which consisted of beef medallions and all the fixings, was delicious and we thoroughly enjoyed ourselves. The program included speeches, jokes, singing, and dancing. I even sang a song that I wrote to Janet. Don gave us a book, entitled *The Virtues of Marriage*. It was a small book. All the pages were empty.

SEVEN

The Trip of a Lifetime

WE WERE EXTREMELY TIRED THE NEXT DAY. WE ORDERED ROOM SERVICE but could hardly eat.

The day after that, we rose early to catch our flight to Hawaii. Our stopover in Chicago was followed by a long flight to Honolulu, after which we boarded another plane for the short flight to Maui. From the airport, we embarked on a long drive to the other side of the island where we had booked a luxurious condo with all the amenities. While there, we typically ate out once a day, eating dinner at sunset. For the first four days, we mainly slept.

We managed to do a bunch of touristy things in Hawaii—walking on the beach, taking tours by train, and going to shops. We even rented a car for a couple of days since I wanted to go up to the observatory at the top of mountain. For Janet, this was a white-knuckled ride up and an even whiter-knuckled ride down.

For me, I loved the scenery. The countryside was lush and green and the view from the top of the volcano was amazing. At ten thousand feet, the air was significantly colder than at sea level. The sky was beautifully clear, and we could see the clouds hovering over the ocean below.

I had brought a guitar with us on our trip. In fact, I don't think I ever went anywhere without a musical instrument of some kind. We loved to sing together.

The first Sunday in Hawaii, we visited a nearby church. An attendee told us that a wedding was to be held there, and they needed someone to sing, so we volunteered. It was a small, intimate Hawaiian wedding, complete with a circle of flowers which the couple stepped into to say their vows. We were able to bless them with the house blessing song. This was a highlight of our time there.

The trip home was arduous. Once again, we drove across the island to the small airport. We then flew in a small plane to Honolulu. From there, we flew back to the continent with another stopover in Chicago. This turned into a long layover and hadn't been in our original plans, but there we were.

Finally, we arrived in Toronto, weary from a long day of travel and lugging all our baggage as well as the treasures we had accumulated. We even brought back a few pineapples to give to our friends. The fruit in Hawaii was so delicious. My favourite food there was the macadamia nuts. Wow! My mouth waters just thinking about it.

Now our real life together began. We were home, in our small apartment, and back to work on Monday.

EIGHT

Life Before Children

FROM THE VERY BEGINNING OF OUR RELATIONSHIP, WE WEREN'T
interested in having children. Reflecting on that, I now believe an ele-
ment of fear controlled us. We knew it was important to establish our
relationship before we introduced the responsibility of children, and it
took a good six years to dispel that fear.

Our first years were blissful. We enjoyed doing everything together while learning more about each other. Physically, we were always
close, sitting together and holding hands. In fact, we were often called
"the hot Daviaus."

Janet was a complete neat freak. If there was a piece of paper
on the floor, the place was a dive. I, on the other hand, did not even
notice such things (I still don't). If there was one thing I was picky
about, it was that everything needed to be in its rightful place, so I
could remember where it was and not have to go looking for it.

By the end of 1981, it was clear that Janet wasn't handling full-
time work very well, as she was exhausted. By the end of the year, she

took a break from working outside the home, but it didn't take long for her to become bored. After that, she held various part-time jobs, from office work to retail.

In September 1982, the church we had been attending fell apart; unfortunately, there were many disputes that couldn't be resolved. People took sides and hostility took over. Eventually, the church held a vote and the pastor was asked to leave. We were among those who stayed with the pastor, but it wasn't the same. Gone was the beautiful, nurturing family we had so enjoyed.

It took a little while, but over time the group that had stayed with the pastor dispersed, and we found ourselves in a spiritual wilderness with no direction for our lives. We still had a few friends but no spiritual family. However, we didn't give up. Instead we went out searching for the right community for us. A couple of places showed promise, but they weren't like the family we had experienced.

In August 1984, just before her fifty-ninth birthday, my mother Germene suddenly passed away. She had always had nagging health issues, and this time she had a stroke and never regained consciousness. We rushed up to Timmins to see her, and three days later she was gone.

Around that time, I started taking classical guitar lessons from Scott, a teacher from the same studio where Leona Boyd had studied. I had an inexpensive guitar and it soon became evident that I needed something better. Scott sent me to the workshop of Sergei de Jonge, who had a guitar sitting around whose original owner hadn't liked it for some reason. Sergei gave me a great deal. According to my teacher, the guitar was one of the best Sergei had ever made.

At the time of this writing, Sergei is still making guitars and teaching others how to create quality instruments.

When starting to learn any instrument, my advice is to search out a good teacher. I had been playing guitar for fifteen years or so, self-taught, and I had to unlearn many things because my technique was completely wrong. I continued taking lessons for about three years, then decided to take Conservatory exams and managed to get to Grade Eight. After that, I started looking at the Grade Nine curriculum, but I didn't like the music. Also, the technical requirements were very challenging. I would have had to practice three hours a day, every day, for at least six months in order to attain that level. I had a life. It wasn't that important for me to have that piece of paper, so I stopped taking lessons.

I didn't abandon the guitar, however. To this day, I still play in a classical style. I continue to keep my nails in shape for playing, short on the left hand and long on the right.

In 1985, shortly after I acquired the guitar, we bought a small, two-bedroom house on Denton Avenue in Scarborough. The bedrooms were tiny, and we decided, with the help of some friends, to convert the house into a one-bedroom. This didn't affect the value of the home, as it almost doubled in two years.

While living on Denton, we had a friend from England named Glynn who stayed with us for a couple of months. During this season, being in a spiritual wasteland, Glynn was a great encouragement. His wife Norma eventually came as well and we remained good friends until they moved back to England many years later.

Two years after moving into our home in Scarborough, we relocated to Pickering and found ourselves close to the commuter train. I worked downtown at one of the telephone companies, and the house was only a ten-minute walk to the station. It took me about an hour to get to work.

I remember the feeling of rest and settling as we established ourselves in our third home. This shift in the atmosphere changed our thinking about children.

NINE

Family Life

A FEW MONTHS AFTER MOVING TO PICKERING, WE FOUND OUT THAT we were expecting our first child. During the months of waiting, we prepared the nursery and had lots of baby showers. Everything was in place—the nursery, the rocking chair, the cradle I had made, and the baby clothes.

Janet was glowing as she grew bigger throughout the nine months. We went to prenatal classes that coached us for labour and delivery. I remember singing and speaking to our baby from outside the womb, saying, "Mummy and Daddy are waiting for you. We love you!"

Janet went into labour early Saturday morning on June 11, 1988. I wasn't home. Nancy, our birthing coach, and her husband Doug were having a garage sale that day and I had stayed at their place overnight to help. Nancy and I hurried back to our house to take Janet to the hospital because her water had already broken.

After we arrived at the hospital, the labour went on hold with nothing really happening. About an hour later, the doctor decided to induce, after which he went for dinner. Labour began again around 6:00 p.m., and before he could return Adelle was born. At 9:30 p.m., another doctor stepped in to handle the delivery. Adelle was a healthy six pounds, eleven ounces. Janet had to have some stitches, but apart from being exhausted from twenty hours of labour, she was fine. I didn't hand out cigars, but I seem to recall that chocolate was involved. Nancy was such a great help to us during that season.

Adelle's birth brought out the child in me, or maybe the lack of sleep affected my brain. We have a picture of me lying in bed with a bright orange golf ball balanced on my forehead. For Christmas, I bought a train set for her. I don't think she particularly cared about trains, but I did because they were so much part of my childhood. By then, I was pretty much a big kid trying to get the little kid in me to come out. I have fond memories of holding her in my arms and walking the floor with her when she was fussy.

My mother had passed away in 1983, and before Adelle was born my dad had gotten remarried to a woman named Carol. He was excited about his first grandchild. They came to visit several times in the next three years. It still warms my heart to remember him holding Adelle on his shoulder and gently patting her back. We enjoy the videos we have of them together.

Dad developed an aggressive form of lung cancer and passed away in October 1991, a few months after Adelle turned three. That was a painful time. I still miss him.

Our daughter didn't crawl much. All of a sudden, at thirteen months, she just got up and started walking. No more sitting around for her.

A couple of memories stand out, like the time she fell asleep in her highchair, face down in spaghetti. She also went through a period of time when she often used the expression "I want." Late one evening we were out driving and the moon was out. I asked her if she wanted the moon. "Want the moon…" and on she went.

On her second birthday, we bought her a Flintstones car. She shook with excitement, got in the car, and drove it around the room.

When Adelle was two and a half, my dad's wife Carol gave her a doll for Christmas that was twice her size. She was overwhelmed and said, "Dolly!" We kept the doll aside for a year or so because it was just too big for her.

We had been reading to her since she was seven months old. Because of this, she soon began speaking fluently. People were astonished at her vocabulary. By the time she was four, she could read simple board books. I still remember her lining stuffed animals up against the couch and reading stories to them like a teacher.

When Adelle was very young, I started doing contract work, which meant frequent trips out of town. My primary client had offices in Mississauga and Montreal, and I often spent Monday through Friday away, either flying to Montreal or taking a limo to the airport. I had a couple of favourite places to stay—Le Grand in Montreal and Embassy Suites by the airport. The money was good, but the expenses were high. Eventually, the contract with the telephone company ended and I found myself out of work.

I had this concept of creating reliable computer applications, and being the adventurous person I am I formed a company with a couple of friends. That venture didn't go as well as I'd hoped, and I spent eleven months with no income. Still, the Lord was faithful and provided for all our needs. The concept I developed worked, but by then some of the larger corporations in the software world had come out with more advanced technology, and our company folded.

Thankfully, I got another contract with a different telephone company, but by then our funds were depleted and our credit was stretched to the limit. We could have kept the house and paid everything off eventually, but we decided that getting out of debt was more important. After selling the house, we moved to a rental in Ajax.

The commute from north Ajax to downtown Toronto was a long one. I had to catch a bus to the train station. Fortunately, the company was close to Union Station. I did contract work there for eight years and then was an employee for another nine years.

When Adelle was around one year old, we started attending Covenant Christian Church, which had a strong small-group community. The notion of belonging to a family returned. Pastor Paul had come from Halifax to establish a ministry in Toronto, and the church met in a school in the north of the city. The drive from Pickering didn't take long, and we only went in on Sundays. The sense of community was refreshing.

During that time, I learned how to lead a small group meeting. I had a passion to lead worship, and I loved to teach. Leading worship with people who come ready is very easy, but the style of teaching in the context of small community groups is very different. There is no monologue for forty-five minutes. Instead we had guided discussions, and it was important to encourage everyone to speak. Sometimes the challenge was getting someone to stop speaking so the others could participate. These group meetings also involved praying for each other.

The meetings at our house were amazing. We had the privilege of hosting two of the pastors' families. Wow! Imagine leading that kind of group!

Adelle is very compassionate towards those with disabilities. My blind friend Ken came for a visit. This is the same Ken who visited me in the hospital with a braille Bible. Adelle showed genuine interest in him and took the initiative to lead him around and get him anything he needed.

Adelle took an interest in art in Grade One and had help from another artistic student. She has excelled greatly in art over the years, and we have a few of her pieces adorning our walls. What a treasure! She also loved animals and still does to this day. Her first pet was a budgie, which was followed by guinea pigs. She got her first puppy when she was sixteen; she named him Grizzly because he looked like a bear cub. She also had fish. She took horseback riding lessons for three years and loved it. Her favourite horse was named Lucy.

From the time Adelle was born until David arrived, Janet had two miscarriages. This was emotionally difficult for both of us. Fortunately, we had friends who supported and encouraged us through that time.

In February 1992, Janet became pregnant again, and David was born on November 12, 1992, shortly after the Blue Jays won their first World Series. It only took three hours from the time Janet started labour until he was born. Once again, the doctor didn't make it on time, and a nurse assisted with the delivery. I was stunned and in shock to watch him come into the world before my very eyes.

David seemed to grow quickly. He was walking by the time he was nine months, and it was evident from early on that he was gifted athletically. Even at a young age, he could kick a moving ball. From what I observed of other children, this wasn't ordinary, and he could hit a ball with a bat very early in life.

When David was still a baby, we moved again. This time, we bought a house in Pickering. We were there for only two years as the value of the house dropped. Over time, we sold and moved into a rental home in North York.

I have many fond memories of the things I did with David. For example, when he was young, we would play with a small frisbee. One time he jumped to catch it and flipped over into a bin of doll clothes. We both laughed.

One of his favourite expressions was, "Play with me, Dad!" And play we did. In the winter, it was ball hockey in the family room downstairs. We set up little nets that were just the right size so we could shoot a ball across the room while still guarding our own net. In the summer, it was baseball, and we used a whiffle ball for that.

One day when he was five or six, David, Adelle, and I went to the North York Centre. Outside one of the entrances, a bunch of steel posts had been set into the cement, a little less than one metre apart. They were probably six inches (fifteen centimetres) in diameter with rounded cement caps on the top, about three feet high. David climbed to the top of the first one and jumped to the next, landing securely. Then he jumped to the next and the next, to the end of the row, never losing his balance. It's a good thing Janet wasn't there; she would most likely have freaked out and stopped him from ever trying such a stunt. That was definitely one of the most athletic things I've ever seen anyone do.

David started T-ball when he was five or six and continued to play baseball for various teams until he was twelve. He was a pitcher and could hit the ball well. At the end of one of our practices at which David had been whacking the ball, one of the members of the adult team came onto the field and said, "Can he come and play for us?"

David eventually lost heart with baseball, after his team lost in the final of the AA Ontario championship. He had been pitching well in that game, but errors in the field prevented them from winning. That was some season.

After baseball came soccer. He started with an indoor team and was an excellent goalkeeper. In his first season, he started with six scoreless games. This was significant because, in indoor soccer, the scores are usually quite high and the game fast-paced. He could throw the ball to the box of the opposing keeper, and they even scored that way a couple of times. At the end of that season, he joined an outdoor team.

David also played the drums. He was pretty good at it, being a well-coordinated person. The day we moved into the house in Don Mills, the drums were the first thing to get set up. He played with the window open, and one particular neighbour took exception to the noise and let us know. David drummed with his window closed from then on.

David learned to play the guitar in his early teens. He never took a lesson but got very good at it. He even took a high school music class and learned to play the piano. He excelled at whatever instrument he played.

Even though Adelle and David were quite different, I thoroughly enjoyed everything I did with them.

We lived on Longmore Street in North York for ten years, continuing to attend Covenant Christian Church (CCC). We eventually bought another house in the Don Mills and Steeles area. I was still working downtown and the commute was long—an hour and twenty minutes each way.

During the years when Adelle and David were growing, we were blessed and privileged to experience and participate in the Toronto Blessing. The Holy Spirit came suddenly in January 1994 and people came from all over the world to experience a fresh fire from heaven.

Our first encounter came during the summer of that year. Our family went to summer camp in Stayner, Ontario, where we were powerfully touched by the Holy Spirit every day. We continued to go to the airport fellowship on Friday nights and for conferences. They continued having meetings six nights a week for twelve years, and millions came from around the world.

We attended CCC until 2002, when we decided to join some family friends, the Macs, in a new church plant. We helped Pastor Rob for about four years and then moved on. The decision to join them was largely mine. I asked the family for their feelings, and no one said anything against it—at least, not until much later. I can't say that staying with CCC would have been better, but hindsight is always twenty-twenty, especially when things don't go as planned.

TEN
Brian

ONE TIME, WHILE STILL LIVING IN THE CITY, WE WERE INVITED TO HOST A foundations class put on by Catch the Fire (CTF) Scarborough. This weekly class covered the basics of faith and spanned approximately fourteen weeks. We opened our home, and about ten total strangers came. We instantly knit together, forming bonds of friendship and love. It was definitely a good experience.

During this time, we met Brian. He is no ordinary man. In his professional life, he's an expert in taking care of ice for curling rinks. However, what makes him a champion is that he is unusually gifted with a rare tenderness and humility. Great in faith, he constantly encourages those around him to be the best they can be. I always felt loved and completely accepted around him.

For a couple of years, I had been meeting with several men on Mondays for worship and hearing God's voice, but that season ended. Brian invited me to join his small group. This was indeed a life-changing experience. Within the context of a small group, we shared the Word and ministered to each other.

At this small group, I was encouraged to not only hear God's voice but also share what I heard with those around me. I hadn't recognized that gift in myself until someone else dug it out and put it on display. This demonstrates the power of mentoring. This was a marvellous season where we gathered weekly with other hungry souls and gave and received encouragement.

Why was attending this group such a life-changing experience? Well, to begin with, I was greatly encouraged by the brothers and sisters. But the most significant part of the experience was the reinforcement of my belief that small community groups are an essential component of successful living.

In this context of small intimate gatherings, true friendships develop and faith grows. If all you do is attend a church service once a week, you are missing out on a lot. The large congregational meeting serves as a place of celebration where we gather in unity, worshipping and serving one another.

However, small community groups provide a meaningful connection with other like-minded believers. Gifts can be discovered, encouraged, and put into use. If you don't belong to a small group of like-minded believers, find one. Make sure that it is a place of encouragement. It will change your life.

ELEVEN
Newmarket

IN THE FALL OF 2007, I WAS APPROACHED BY A LONGTIME FRIEND concerning the company he worked for. He told me that they needed help with a project to speed up their web interface. Since I had experience in that field, I offered to take a look.

I soon met with Mr. B. and we came up with a plan of attack. It quickly became evident that the issues required full-time attention, so I quit my steady, full-time job with a telephone company to join this startup under contract.

In 2008, the trouble started. Money wasn't coming in from sales and the company's investors were running out of resources. For quite a while, we didn't get paid. Even though this was a stressful time, the Lord continued to provide for our needs.

I should have run, but I didn't. I firmly believed that the product was good and worth pursuing, even though my involvement with the company took my family to the brink of financial disaster. We borrowed against the house and deferred certain payments.

In 2010, a new investor came on the scene, promising us steady pay. However, the money we received was only a portion of the amount initially promised.

In 2011, the office moved to Newmarket. For a while, I commuted with a coworker. When that ended, I took public transit. It was a long commute, one and a half hours each way, and that was with someone meeting me at the bus. Without that contact, it would have taken two hours each way.

Thankfully, I was able to work from home on Mondays and Fridays and stayed overnight in Newmarket with one of the owners Tuesdays and Wednesdays. Janet would come and pick me up in Newmarket at the end of the day on Thursday.

By 2012, in the midst of severe financial strain, we decided to sell our house and move to Newmarket. Adelle chose to stay in Toronto. She found a place and moved into shared accommodation.

Repairs needed to be done to the house before we could sell it. Fortunately, we had a lot of help from our CTF Scarborough friends, who willingly gave of their time. By selling the house, we were able to get out of debt and start over. Once again, we rented. David, who had recently graduated from high school, came to live with us.

How we got the house was quite miraculous. One of our friends in Newmarket knew we were looking for a place and had spread the word among his friends. One day, a stranger called to let us know there was a house for rent on Gorham Street. We made an appointment and went to see it. Loving the beautiful four-bedroom, three-bathroom home from the start, we applied right away and were quickly approved. I now had only a twenty-minute walk to the office. We were debt-free and ready to rebuild.

David was offered a job at a rock-climbing gym in Newmarket through a youth pastor who worked there. This was a life-altering experience for him. He hadn't done any rock-climbing in the past, but he quickly learned the ropes. Over the next four or five years, he became a coach and helped many young people learn how to climb. He also learned how to set the walls. In fact, he went to British Columbia and was trained in this by some of the best in the world, which opened a lot of doors for him.

By 2015, it became increasingly difficult to get glasses made for me because of the thickness of my prescription. After consulting with my ophthalmologist, it was agreed that cataract surgery would alleviate the problem. I went through the process with one of Ontario's leading eye surgeons. The operation took place in May and June 2016 with good results.

However, although the surgery was a complete success, my effective eyesight was still about the same. My glasses are now much thinner and easier to acquire.

In the early summer of 2016, Adelle and her dog Grizzly moved in with us. She continued to do bookkeeping as well as create a lot of art on the side, which is her real passion. She filled her room with artwork from floor to ceiling. It was a pleasure to see her creativity flow.

On Labour Day of 2017, while working in the garage with my brother Gene, an electric tool slipped, causing a serious injury to my left pinkie. I had surgery three days later and wore a cast for eight weeks, following by another five weeks of physiotherapy.

The ER doctor had told me I would never play the guitar again. However, I was playing again by the next summer, mostly because of the prompting of our church's worship leader. In addition, I completed the guitar I had been building when the accident happened.

As always, even through hard times, God was faithful as we followed His leading and trusted in Him.

TWELVE
The Message

EVERY LIFE HAS MEANING, EVERY LIFE HAS VALUE, AND EVERY PERSON has a story. Mine is no different. Thinking back over the past sixty-eight years, I know I am different today than when I was a child. Yes, my body grew up—and out—but much more than that has changed. As a younger person, I was a shy and timid.

The stigma of disability initially affected my character. Despite this so-called disability, I completed college and developed an amazing career. I married a wonderful woman who is a constant encouragement to me. I have two amazingly gifted children whom I love very much.

Is that all there is—you live, you change, you...? No, I have not finished my race.

There have been recurring themes in my life that I am sure will continue, such as the theme of being healed from life's wounds, the theme of redemption into relationship with God and others, and helping others to experience the same.

Yes, my family experience was fractured when I started school. Being disconnected from my family had far greater significance than my disability. I've had a strong tendency to turn inward and become reclusive, and there's a part of me that still prefers solitude. However, God has, again and again, connected me with people—members of His family. These precious ones have nurtured and encouraged me throughout my life.

This process continues today. I continue to give and receive. People come and go. The point is not how long a friendship lasts but that the positive impact we have on each other while we are connected.

I have a story to tell, but who is this message intended for? I'm not sure, but if you are reading this, don't stop. The purpose of my life is not defined by the events I have experienced. The message, the meaning, is what God has done in my life in freeing me to be what He has created me to be.

By the grace of God, and with the help of the Holy Spirit, I have overcome the fractures of my childhood. The pain of my past is still there, but they no longer define me. I've made peace with past traumas. I'm free from the clutches of pain, free to not only talk and be transparent but to help others who are going through the same thing.

If I had to boil it down to a single message, it would be this: find a meaningful, faith-filled community and connect to it. Make sure that it is a place of honour and respect. Without this, the community will only bring more pain. Be willing to open your heart. Be prepared to give, as much as you can. Be willing to receive. There will be bumps and grinds along the way, but the Lord will take you by the hand and walk with you through it all.

Before I talk about the power of meaningful Christian community in more detail, though, I would like to present two essential truths.

First, because healing starts with God Himself, it is essential to get connected with Him, His way. Therefore, I must present the message of the gospel. Second, because it is impossible to maintain long-lasting meaningful relationships with others without forgiveness, I must talk about it.

THIRTEEN
The Eternal

I GREW UP IN A VERY RELIGIOUS ENVIRONMENT. I KNEW ALL ABOUT THE things I needed to do in order to be pleasing to God, but I had no relationship with Him. In my teens, my heart searched for more.

When Ken shared with me the message of God's love in Jesus, my view of God changed forever. My life since then has been a constant process of change. I have learned to rely completely on God and His Holy Spirit. I continue to learn, particularly in the areas of demonstrating love and patience towards others. And now I know I am not an orphan but a beloved son of God, and heaven is my home.

The message of the gospel is so simple that it takes childlike faith to understand it. God made it that way so that anyone who believes can become His child.

John 1:11–12 says, *"He came to that which was his own, but his own did not receive him. Yet to all who did receive him, to those who believed in his name, he gave the right to become children of God…"*

God's love never fails (1 Corinthians 13:8). In His love, He has faithfully reached out to me. His love has formed a golden thread throughout my life. Love is God's primary nature. This is who He is.

John writes, *"Dear friends, let us love one another, for love comes from God. Everyone who loves has been born of God and knows God. Whoever does not love does not know God, because God is love"* (1 John 4:7–8).

When I was presented with the good news about God, I knew that I needed Him. Genesis 1:27 tells us that God created man in His own image. We were created to know Him.

As a teen, I was filled with insecurity from years of pain and rejection. I didn't know who I was. The emptiness in me called out to be filled, and I longed to be free. Like many my age, I was searching. I longed to be loved unconditionally and valued for who I was. I didn't go crazy with all sorts of wild behaviour, because I was always afraid of punishment. I frequently turned into the class clown, but that only brought temporary attention. I was still lonely and empty. There was a void in my heart that only the love of God could fill.

Here is where God in His mercy comes in. Isaiah states, *"We all, like sheep, have gone astray, each of us has turned to our own way; and the Lord has laid on him the iniquity of us all"* (Isaiah 53:5).

Notice the word *all*. We have *all* gone astray. And here is the beautiful mystery of the gospel. The Lord has laid on Him the iniquity (rebellion) and sin of us all. Who is this *Him* whom the prophet Isaiah spoke of? It is Jesus.

> *Yet to all who did receive him, to those who believed in his name, he gave the right to become children of God—*

children born not of natural descent, nor of human decision or a husband's will, but born of God. (John 1:12–13)

God made him who had no sin to be sin for us, so that in him we might become the righteousness of God. (2 Corinthians 5:21)

This is love: not that we loved God, but that he loved us and sent his Son as an atoning sacrifice for our sins. (1 John 4:10)

So here is the great exchange. God took the judgment for all our sins and laid it upon Jesus. Jesus took upon Himself our sins and died for them so that we would not have to be punished. As a result, we can now have right standing with God by believing in Jesus. He removed the shame and fear of death that had control of us. In receiving Him, we are now being made into the image of God.

Jesus has given us all the choice to either receive or reject Him. Accepting Jesus means accepting His perfect gift of eternal life and recognizing that we can't earn right standing with God through our own effort.

Paul writes, *"For it is by grace you have been saved, through faith—and this is not from yourselves, it is the gift of God—not by works, so that no one can boast"* (Ephesians 2:8–9).

If you choose to accept this incomprehensible gift, try this prayer, saying it out loud:

Jesus, I recognize that I need you. Without You, part of me is missing. I believe that You surrendered Your life on the cross to take away all my sin and shame. I believe that You rose from the dead so that I can have eternal life with You. I freely surrender my heart and life to You. Come and transform me from the inside out. Thank You, Lord!

When I said a prayer similar to this, my heart was changed from being bound in religion to being free by His grace. This was not based on anything I had done, but what Jesus and the Holy Spirit has done in me. The transformation was gradual, and I am still a work in progress.

Now, having opened the door to a life of fellowship with the Father, Son, and Holy Spirit, it is important that you connect with others who are actively seeking to have their hearts transformed. Ask the Holy Spirit to connect you with those who want to have a deep, authentic connection with God and His children.

Also, ask Him to align you with those whom He would have you travel on your spiritual journey. Find a local church where the gospel of Jesus is preached and the love of God is flowing within the congregation and out to the community.

Begin reading the Bible. A good place to start is the gospels—Matthew, Mark, Luke, and John. The book of Romans is also an excellent book to focus on, as are the rest of the writings of Paul the Apostle.

FOURTEEN
Forgiveness

FORGIVENESS IS CENTRAL TO THE GOSPEL. MANY HAVE WRITTEN GREAT volumes about it, and I am not about to reproduce their work. I simply want to point out some of the basic principles that surround it. Similar to my salvation, I can testify about how forgiveness affected my life.

When I was young, I experienced a lot of difficulties in my life which caused me to become angry. I wasn't the type to explode, yelling and screaming at people—I simply held it all inside. That meant that I lived with internal agitation.

It wasn't until I heard teaching by Dr. Larry Lee that I learned how important it was to end the cycle of bitterness. He taught that we have to make a decision, on a daily basis, not only to forgive past hurts but to live in an attitude where every offence is forgiven on the spot.

I even made a poster to remind myself to do this. It said, "Today, I choose to forgive everyone, everything." Over time, my attitude towards people and life in general became a lot more relaxed and peaceful on the inside.

So let's have a look at three central aspects of forgiveness.

RECEIVING

The first step, of course, is that we have to receive forgiveness from God. In the previous chapter, we learned that none of us can measure up to God's standard. Recall Paul's words in Romans: *"all have sinned and fall short of the glory of God"* (Romans 3:23). That is why we need His forgiveness and to know that we are forgiven. Knowing this frees us from the guilt for everything we have ever done wrong.

Romans also affirms, *"Therefore, there is now no condemnation for those who are in Christ Jesus, because through Christ Jesus the law of the Spirit who gives life has set you free from the law of sin and death"* (Romans 8:1–2).

Imagine that! God Himself said through the apostle that there is no condemnation to those who are in Christ Jesus. If you look at the verses at the end of Romans 7, you will see that Paul, the author of these words, was struggling with his inadequacies. Here is the man who wrote half of the New Testament, struggling. Out of that struggle came the words "no condemnation" (Romans 8:1).

In Colossians, Paul also says, *"For he has rescued us from the dominion of darkness and brought us into the kingdom of the Son he loves, in whom we have redemption, the forgiveness of sins"* (Colossians 1:13–14).

We were rescued out of the kingdom of darkness. We were in darkness because of our sin nature. In Hebrews 9:22, we read that only through the shedding of blood can sins be remitted.

Ephesians confirms this: *"In him we have redemption through his blood, the forgiveness of sins, in accordance with the riches of*

God's grace that he lavished on us. With all wisdom and under-standing…" (Ephesians 1:7–8)

Matthew reveals Jesus's words: *"This is my blood of the cove-nant, which is poured out for many for the forgiveness of sins"* (Matthew 26:28).

So now, because He took all our sin and paid the penalty for it with His own blood, we are free to receive His complete forgiveness.

GIVING

Having received forgiveness, it is now imperative that we practice forgiving others. In the Lord's Prayer, Jesus tells us something significant about forgiveness. In Matthew, He prays, *"And forgive us our debts, as we also have forgiven our debtors"* (Matthew 6:12).

He reminds us again, *"For if you forgive other people when they sin against you, your heavenly Father will also forgive you. But if you do not forgive others their sins, your Father will not forgive your sins"* (Matthew 6:14–15).

When we refuse to forgive, we are passing judgment on others. Jesus told us not to judge. With any judgment we put on others, we bring judgment onto ourselves. If we want mercy from the Father, we need to extend mercy.

Matthew tells us, *"Do not judge, or you too will be judged. For in the same way you judge others, you will be judged, and with the measure you use, it will be measured to you"* (Matthew 7:1–2).

Luke instructs us, *"Be merciful, just as your Father is merciful"* (Luke 6:36).

Other scriptures also instruct us to forgive. Mark says, *"And when you stand praying, if you hold anything against anyone, forgive* them, so that your Father in heaven may forgive you your sins" (Mark 11:25).

Holding on to unforgiveness is like drinking poison and hoping the person you hold a grudge against dies. In fact, forgiving someone else benefits you more than the other person. God Himself chose this path for His own sake. As He confirms in Isaiah, *"I, even I, am he who blots out your transgressions, for my own sake, and remembers your sins no more"* (Isaiah 43:25).

Here are more scriptures that encourage us to forgive:

Be kind and compassionate to one another, forgiving each other, just as in Christ God forgave you. (Ephesians 4:32)

Bear with each other and forgive one another if any of you has a grievance against someone. Forgive as the Lord forgave you. (Colossians 3:13)

Next is this question: how do you forgive someone who has hurt you deeply? As with everything, forgiveness must be accomplished by faith and through the help of the Holy Spirit. It's not something we can do by simply making a mental decision. Yes, we have to make the decision, but our decision must be supported by the help and grace that Jesus pours out on us through His Holy Spirit.

Sometimes hurts go deep, being passed down from generation to generation. Hatred can be inherited to the point where someone might not even know he hates; it's just there. The key to freedom is to realize that when you accept Jesus, you become a new person.

Your old nature has died and you take on the new nature of Christ living in you.

In 2 Corinthians 5:17, we read, *"Therefore, if anyone is in Christ, the new creation has come: the old has gone, the new is here!"*

Indeed, you are now free to be part of the family of God. As John writes,

> *Yet to all who did receive him, to those who believed in his name, he gave the right to become children of God— children born not of natural descent, nor of human decision or a husband's will, but born of God.* (John 1:12–13)

So because you are born again into a new family, into a new culture, into the Kingdom of God, you are free to leave the ancestral hurts behind. Once you forgive, you will experience true freedom. Hatred and hostility produce death in us. Love, powered by unconditional forgiveness, produces life.

LIVING

Life is filled with all kinds of opportunities to take offence. In general, there are three types of hurt that can come our way.

First of all, most of the time people do things out of ignorance. That's not to say they are dumb; they are simply unaware that their actions are offensive to others.

As an example, I remember someone telling me that they thought dipping bread in the soft yoke of an egg was disgusting. To that person, the way I love to eat my eggs is offensive.

In our multicultural society, we are exposed to the habits, good or bad, of different cultures, and of course we all have different personalities, likes, and dislikes. We have a choice to make. What do we do with these offences which are not intentionally committed again us?

Here is what Solomon, the wisest man who ever lived, says in Proverbs: *"A person's wisdom yields patience; it is to one's glory to overlook an offense"* (Proverbs 19:11).

Within the body of Christ, we can live above these everyday cultural and personality differences because we are all united in Christ. We do this by maintaining an attitude of forgiveness.

Some people call this tolerance. I don't like that word because it implies putting up with someone, burying the hurts.

I know it is possible, with the help of the Holy Spirit, to truly live at peace with each other. Love covers a multitude of sins (Proverbs 10:12, 1 Peter 4:8). One thing that helps greatly with this is spending time in the presence of the Lord, soaking up His love. When we do this consistently, we will be less likely to take or hold onto offences.

Our families give us plenty of opportunities to practice this. If we were perfect parents, we would have perfect children. But the opposite is closer to reality. We come into this world as children of broken parents. We grow up broken, have our children, pass our brokenness onto them, and the cycle continues.

In Christ, that cycle is broken. As we embrace the forgiveness of Christ, we are able to extend that to our parents and children, breaking the generational chains and setting ourselves and our children free to live unhindered by the sins of the past. When love and forgiveness is added to the family, everything changes. This is how strong families are built.

The second way in which offences occur is through actions that are not casual but deliberate. People can, for one reason or other, deliberately seek to cause us harm. Here is where a strength of character and lots of help from the Holy Spirit comes in.

Two things can happen. Sometimes the offending person will ask for forgiveness. Sometimes he or she will repeat the same hurtful actions over and over and continually ask for forgiveness. What do we do with that? The answer can be found in a conversation between Jesus and Peter.

Matthew 18:21–22 says,

Then Peter came to Jesus and asked, "Lord, how many times shall I forgive my brother or sister who sins against me? Up to seven times?"

Jesus answered, "I tell you, not seven times, but seventy-seven times."

A footnote in my Bible says that this could be read as "seventy times seven." If you do the math, that is 490 times. In Luke's account of the same teaching, Jesus says that this is the number of sins which should be forgiven every day (Luke 17:4).

Consider this scenario: someone you know does something hurtful to you and asks forgiveness 490 times in one day. You are to forgive them. Wow! I certainly think I would lose my patience if that were to happen. Yet forgiveness must prevail to keep our hearts soft.

I think it is important to also say something about anger. Anger is a feeling, an emotional response to injustice or hurt. All of us have feelings. They are part of who we are, and they are essential, just as our five physical senses are beneficial. For example, the sense of touch is vital to our existence. Feelings of heat or cold can alert us to danger. The tender embrace of a loved one can comfort us.

In the same way, our emotional senses, of which anger is one, can be beneficial. The anger itself isn't wrong, but how we handle it is important.

Ephesians admonishes us, *"'In your anger do not sin': Do not let the sun go down while you are still angry, and do not give the devil a foothold"* (Ephesians 4:26–27).

Here, Paul instructs us to deal with our anger right away. If we don't, we can give the devil a foothold in our lives. Anger leads to resentment, resentment leads to bitterness, bitterness leads to hostility, and hostility leads to bondage. The bondage of hostility is a stronghold of the enemy. People don't commit acts of violence when they first feel anger; it takes a prolonged meditation on unresolved wounds for violence to ensue.

So what is the benefit of anger?

Tell me something: are you passionate about anything? What makes you get up in the morning, other than your physical needs? Do you have something that drives you, something in the world that you want to see changed? Most likely, that started when you saw some injustice and felt anger.

My dear brothers and sisters, take note of this: Everyone should be quick to listen, slow to speak and slow to become angry, because human anger does not produce the righteousness that God desires. (James 1:19–20)

Here it is, plain and simple: are you going to allow your feelings to control you, becoming enslaved by them, or are you going to take charge and benefit from them? Remember that in the face of injustice or downright hurt, you have a choice. If you see injustice, start by applying forgiveness to the perpetrator, then start praying for the injured.

Finally, because God wants all to be saved, start praying for the one who is causing the hurt. If you are the one being hurt, choose to lay it down. Again, apply forgiveness, pray for the one hurting you, and bless them.

I am not saying that this is easy. We constantly need the help of the Holy Spirit to do this. We must draw near to God.

Submit yourselves, then, to God. Resist the devil, and he will flee from you. Come near to God and he will come near to you. (James 4:7–8)

The key in all areas of life is to stay close to God. His anointing and grace enables us to live victorious lives.

The third area of difficulty we face is caused by temptation and the lies of the enemy. The biggest lie that I face every day is that I am worthless. I think this is a common accusation.

Satan and his demons are the only ones we are not to forgive. We are to make no place for him or his lies. Warfare is being waged in our minds, and the only way to win is by using the Word of the living God.

Here is my confession according to the Word of God: "I am a child of the living God, and that gives me tremendous worth."

FIFTEEN
The Power of Community

AS I REFLECT ON MY LIFE, I HAVE EXPERIENCED NUMEROUS EXPRES-
sions of the Christian community. Most of them were good and positive. All of them have, together, contributed to my identity. It wasn't
so much the people or the circumstances that surrounded these
experiences that changed me, but the context and the framework
of what happened.

I have learned so much about who I am from those around me.
Our identities should indeed be founded only on what Jesus says
about us. Yes, we can read the Word and get a picture of what God
intends for us. However, because we don't always see things clearly,
we most often need other people's perspectives.

True Christian community is the process and result of the relationship between believers who deliberately share life with complete
transparency.

So why is community so important? It is the framework for personal growth. For example, I love to build musical instruments. The
process of building a violin is quite complicated. You don't just walk

up to a maple tree, cut it down, and it becomes a violin. People have been making violins for hundreds of years, and to become a good violin maker you have to learn from those with knowledge, masters who have in turn learned from other masters. A true master teacher does not hold back any "secret tricks," nor does he shun new concepts. The teacher and the student become a team, with a specific goal in mind.

The same is true of our human existence. You don't emerge from the womb walking and talking. You are first created by an act of intimacy between your father and mother. After birth, you are dependent on your parents. You know only one form of communication: crying.

Very quickly, however, the process of learning starts. Most parents start by not knowing what to do with this unique individual, and it is very helpful to find a community of experienced parents. Of course, everybody has free advice to offer. My parents would say, "When I had you, we did things a lot differently, so…" Raising children is challenging at best, and even harder if you are alone.

So what does the family have to do with community? Well, the family is the smallest unit of community and a great example of what true community looks like. Family is where children start learning who they are. In a healthy family context, the loving encouragement of fathers and mothers contribute to a child's identity.

The breakdown of the family today has led to an entire generation of children and young people who have no identity; they are defined solely by what the media says. These lost ones go out to find leaders who will show them who they are. Like the blind leading the blind, the result is disastrous.

The brokenness in society we see today can be fixed, but it is going to take a widespread unfolding of the body of Christ working together to renew the identity of all the lost ones.

True Christian community is like a healthy family with fathers and mothers guiding the way. Every Christian community has a leader or facilitator. They are usually trained and appointed by their mentors. The purpose of the leader is to motivate and encourage, as a good parent would. The leader is generally the one who community members turn to for help and guidance. He or she provides a safe environment for members to learn and grow.

In my experience of leading a small group, I learned just as much as those I was leading. Everyone has a gift, and when all the gifts are allowed to function, everyone benefits, including the leader.

In true Christian community:

1. You receive identity through the affirmation of those around you. Remember, in Christ, you are a valued member of the family.
2. You get and give input to each other, building up each other's faith. Testimony is vital to the Christian experience. It is indisputable because it relates to events, not theories. It demonstrates what is possible in the midst of all the circumstances of life.
3. You find out what your gifts are. Every person has a gift. You may not know what that is until someone else uncovers it for you.

4. You learn to abandon selfishness and self-centeredness. This is important, as giving to others is far more gratifying than receiving.

5. You learn that prayer changes things. When two of you agree, in prayer, concerning something, it will be done (Matthew 18:19).

Just like in a family, respect and a culture of honour are essential in order to have healthy relationships. When there is a breakdown of honour, community stops. Just look at society today—no honour, no respect, and widespread chaos.

Respect and honour don't come naturally; they must be modelled. Love—and God Himself—compels us to respect and honour one another.

CONCLUSION

I AM GOING TO CONTINUE TO PURSUE THE PURPOSE FOR WHICH GOD has put me on this earth. I will continue to run with the message God has put in my heart. We are all partners together in ministry. It is my hope that the course of my life will have brought a change in the course of yours.

Embrace life, embrace love, and embrace God! He is closer than you think.